In the Tin

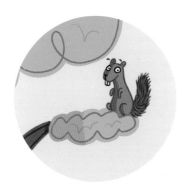

Written by
Jill Atkins

Illustrated by
Ellie O'Shea

Ransom

Dan has a tin can.

The tin can has a lid.

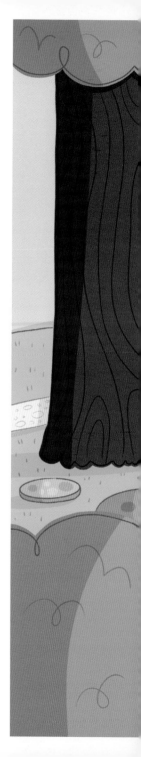

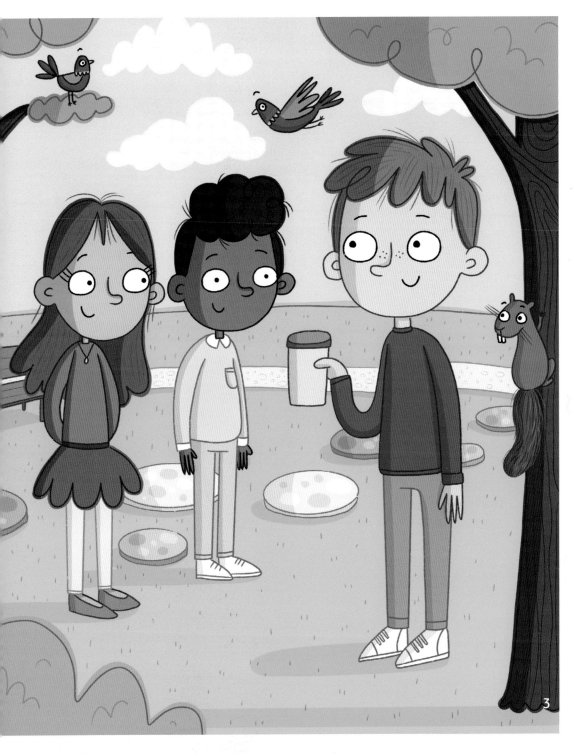

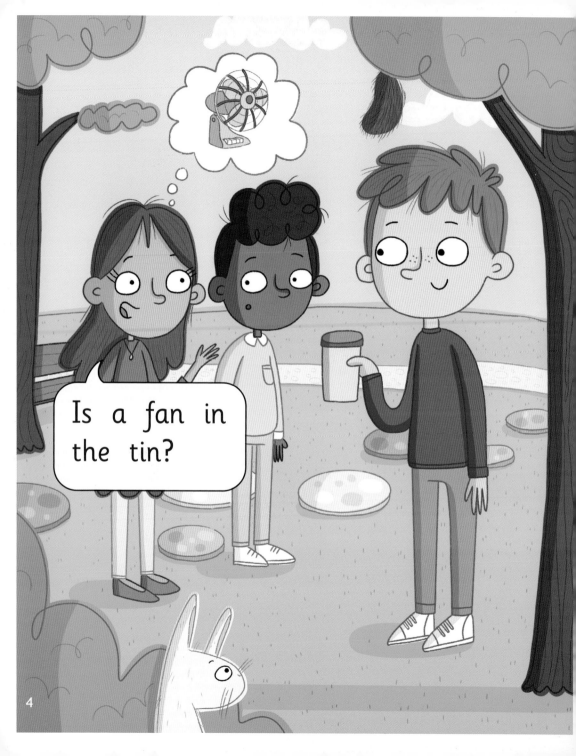

Is a fan in the tin?

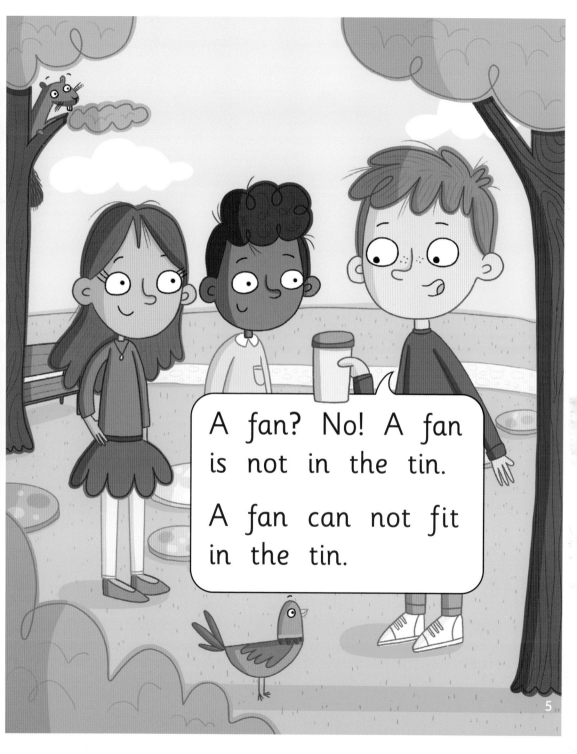

A fan? No! A fan is not in the tin.

A fan can not fit in the tin.

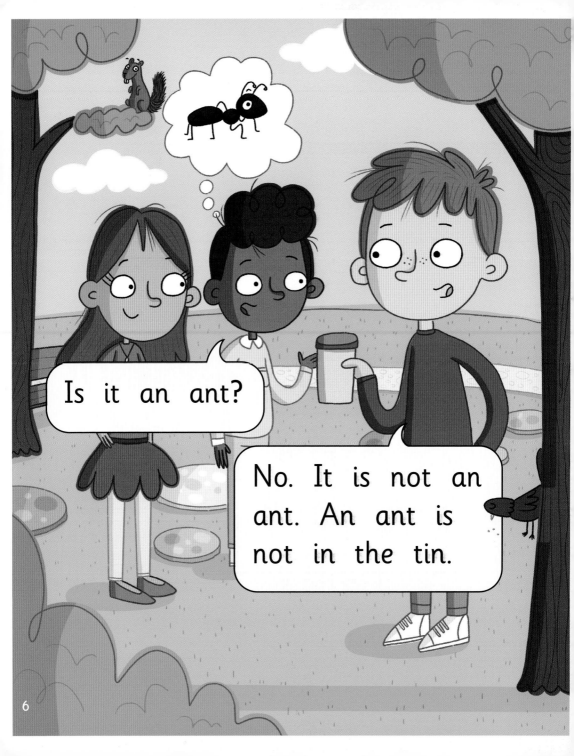

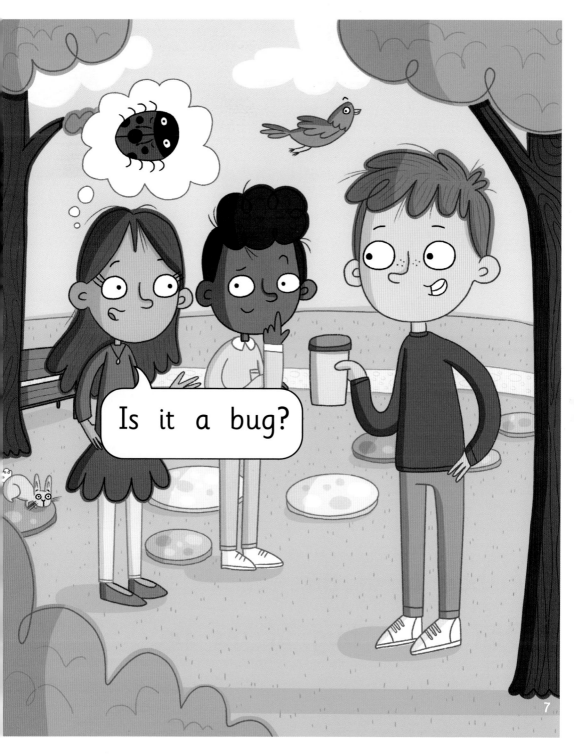

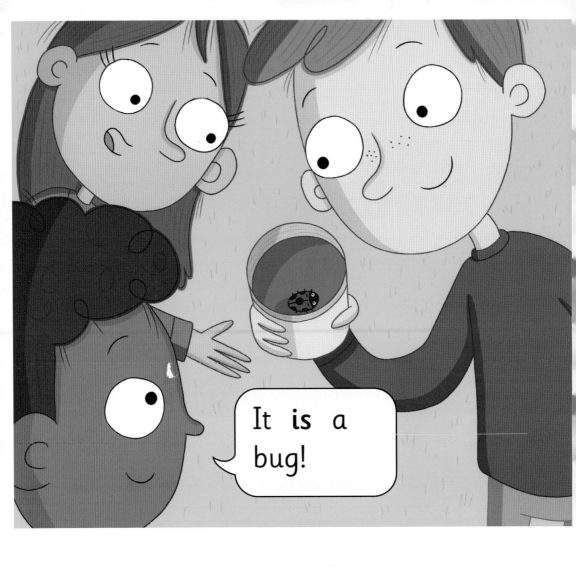

A bug **is** in the tin!

Dan has a bug in the tin.